Refined Jewels

Allowing Pressure to Shape You into Greater from the Inside Out

Kamisha Lattimore

Refined Jewels

Copyright © 2017 Kamisha Lattimore

ALL RIGHTS RESERVED. This book contains material protected under International and Federal Copyright Laws and Treaties. Any unauthorized reprint or use of this material is prohibited. No part of this book may be reproduced or transmitted in any form or by any means, electronic or mechanical, including photocopying, recording, or by any information storage and retrieval system without express written permission from the author / publisher

CONTENTS

Introduction……...............................………..7

Chapter 1 - A Stone Covered:

        The Protection of Love 17

Chapter 2 - Hidden and Set Apart 35

Chapter 3 - Living Above Fear 49

Chapter 4 - Eliminating Distractions 77

Chapter 5 - Adversity to Your Advantage 99

Chapter 6 - Withstanding Fire 117

Chapter 7 - The Beauty in the Breaking 147

Chapter 8 - Shine Bright for His Glory 157

Prayer of Salvation 167

Bonus: Refined Reflections 169

ACKNOWLEDGMENTS

I thank every single person who has helped my journey of Refinement.

Thanks to my mom, the epitome of a Refined Jewel. You have gone through so much molding, shaping, and fire, all to be the beautiful soul you are today. To my sister who has always been there in every single season.

To those who have to overcome battles daily; who have endured pain in their childhood, who have overcome struggles they were too ashamed to share with others. For the adult who is still coming to terms with the story of her life. I wrote this for you. You are not in this moment of your life by chance. You are right where you need to be, and you have the great choice to make your future greater, wiser, and refined.

Introduction

"Invest in the human soul, who knows, it might be a diamond in the rough" - May McLeod Bethune

Are you struggling to remain strong in today's society? Do you find yourself choosing between who you want to be and who God has created you to be? If so, this book will encourage you to stick with the process. As you read, may you be strengthened, empowered, and motivated to trust God more than you ever dared to in the past. If you have built up a wall of protection and filtered your true feelings behind smiles and insecurities or if you have never reached out and asked for help because you may not believe help is there for you, keep reading; you are in for a big surprise. There is so much in store. God is your very present help in time of trouble. When it seems the world has walked out, I assure you my friend, God has already walked in and can work on your behalf. May you awaken with love, strength, confidence, and joy. You are more valuable than you know, more valuable than you understand.

Refined Jewels was manifested out of passion and a whole lot of uncomfortable pressure in my life. Watching people underestimate who they are and what they are worth always makes my heart heavy. Whether it is a lack of care for themselves, negative self-talk or even treating others poorly on a consistent basis because of a reflection of their own self-worth, it is often a sad encounter.

I used to be a very quiet and shy girl in my childhood days but I was also friendly and polite as my mother raised me to be. I can recall times when I was picked on for being so timid. I was never with the "it" crowd. I didn't choose my friends by appearance or popularity. Rather, I was always drawn to people who were genuine, kind, and loyal. It didn't matter to me what kind of clothes they wore or how their hair looked. I loved kind-hearted people.

As I got a little older, I slowly began to allow outside influences to change me. One time in middle school, I became friends with another girl who was neither popular nor was she known by many people but I liked her. So on the first day of school, we hung out, played together at recess, and sat together at lunch. It went on well for about two weeks until another girl in my class pointed me out one day, "Hey girl, come over here with us; leave that nerd chick alone." Just like that, our friendship slowly came to an end. I looked at her with some slight regret but went on to hang out with the girl who was in the "it" crowd.

Of course, now that I am an adult, looking back, I know it was wrong and very immature of me to just stop talking to someone based on what someone else thought about them. What's even more disturbing is that I did it so quickly probably because of how I felt about myself. Had I been confident about who I was, I wouldn't have allowed someone else to tell me who I should befriend. I was just a twelve-year-old girl who wanted to be liked and accepted.

That school year, I went on to become close friends with the popular girl, doing things she did, wearing her kind of clothes and shopping at her type of stores. I was living in another person's shadow instead of being myself boldly and proudly.

Sad to say, many adults in today's world are still doing that very thing. They continue to be who society tells them to be and to do the things society says they should do instead of being set apart and walking on their own journeys.

In my first book, *A Chosen Journey,* I shared the importance of embracing God's plan for your life. If you do it right, there will be many things about your journey that will be very different from others. If you don't accept that early on, you will always try to validate yourself based on the majority, on statistics, and on what's "trending" now.

We have to be confident with being the outlier and learn to be OK being developed behind the scenes instead of thinking the front street is the place to be all the time. I'm reminded of a very profound scripture, "He has made everything beautiful in its time" (Ecclesiastes 3:11). The key word here is "its." In today's world, we try to make things how we want them in our time. Big mistake. We miss out on the process of an amazing journey trying to perfect and control things before they need to happen.

The past year or so, I have been intentionally focused on understanding the value of the process. When I look back over my entire life from birth to now in my 20's, the complete journey was a process and it's still taking place. What's amazing is that I can now comprehend earlier events of my life and their importance in bringing me to where I am today.

As children of God, we are precious jewels. We are very special and important in every way imaginable. God purchased us with a high price. He died on a cross and rose again with all power in His hands so that we could be saved and have a right to life everlasting. That is the first and foremost sight to behold and understand. Do you know anyone else who would lay down his/her life for you? Not many people would do that, even if they tell you they would.

Jesus kept His promise to die for us; therefore, we owe God our lives. We are to respect the value that He has placed on us by living as if we know our worth. In spite of what others may say, it is still possible to do that even in today's world. Furthermore, you don't have to live like someone in ancient times. You can be young, saved, hidden in Christ, and still have the time of your life. Trust me; if I had heard that back in my teenage years, I may not have believed it either but God gives His children grace for every situation. You just have to desire it and believe it is possible for you.

Chapter 1

A STONE COVERED: THE PROTECTION OF LOVE

"Let all that you do be done in love" (1 Corinthians 16:14)

Protection is one of the vital characteristics of love. Anything that is loved and valued is to be kept safe and protected with the utmost security. God's love for us is far too deep for Him to allow everything to enter our lives. I now understand why I couldn't do certain things I wanted to do in my earlier years. While others around me would "get away" with doing what they wanted, the minute I tried, it seemed like something always interfered with my plans or they were canceled. Although we make plans, it is the Lord who allows things to come to fruition. I'm reminded of Proverbs 16:9, "A man's heart plans his way, but the Lord establishes his steps." God's

love is amazing and it will keep you out of danger. A father who loves his daughter does not allow her to hang out with everyone, and he does not let her do as she pleases. Why? He sees beyond her desires; he knows what's best for her. He can see the dangers ahead that she may not even see. In like manner, as an earthly father protects his daughter Christ also protects and loves us, His children.

Growing up without my father in the household definitely impacted me in many ways. I didn't know early what that type of fatherly protection looked like in action. As a result, I didn't exercise proper judgment in certain environments.

Although my mom did an amazing job raising me, she was a woman so there were certain things she could not teach me about the male gender. As I got older, I learned by trial and error when guys showed an interest in me because of the lack of a male influence in my life when I was growing up. Thankfully, I learned that the Lord can be all to us that we think we lack.

As time went on, I began to look to God as that strong father figure. You might be thinking, "How can you do that? How can God help you with making decisions about guys?" Well, He can. His Word is His heart and His mind and so, one of the first steps I made was reading my Bible and gaining an understanding of His love for me. Then I formed a two-way relationship in prayer.

I asked God to lead and guide me into all truth and wisdom. I learned that when we are being led by the Holy Spirit, we will never go astray. Let me explain: when you really decide to live for God, His love covers and protects you. No one will be able to "get over on you." You will not have to develop the world's mentality of being harsh or rude to protect yourself because no one will be able to "play you." I will say this: I was "played"

many times in my life in relationships because I was operating in my own ways and my own will. Once I realized what I was doing was horrible, and I got tired of the same old things, I surrendered that area of my life to God. It made all the difference!

The Bible says, "But when he, the spirit of truth, comes, he will guide you into all truth. He will not speak on his own, he will speak only what he hears, and he will tell you what is yet to come" (John 16:13). When I began to draw closer to God, in return, He began to reveal plans and His heart to me. If I ventured where He did not want me to be, I would sense it wasn't the right place for me. If I was with a guy who had an interest in me, in the midst of the conversation I would ask the right question or start talking about a particular topic. In those moments, I would receive confirmation that he was not a man I should continue spending time with. God is neither a time waster nor is He a Father who wants His children exposed to influences that are unhelpful and damaging to their lives and destinies.

Does this mean that if someone doesn't meet your standards you should avoid them? If a guy doesn't cross all his T's and dot all his I's is it pointless talking to him? No! Make no mistake about what I'm saying; we are all sinners constantly in need of grace and mercy. None of us has arrived so we can't view others with a stuck-up, condescending attitude; however, when it comes to the covenant of marriage and destiny, there are specific types of people God wants His children to be with. Those who love Him and will inspire others to draw closer to Him, not closer to sin and death.

    Everyone comes with a fair share of challenges and shortcomings but the Lord kept me from situations that could have ultimately destroyed me. Thank God for discernment and wisdom.

Many years ago, a young man showed interest in me. At that time, I was serious about honoring God in my relationships, and I did not even want to think of dating anyone who wasn't on the same page as me. In the past, I would operate by my standards; sometimes, I would compromise to be in a relationship with someone because they had other "good" qualities about them. Maybe they were physically attractive, educated, had a fun personality or were just easy to talk to. I would place all those things before the standards God set for me. However, the result was always the same; these relationships would end. I kept asking myself after things did not work out for me, "How do I keep ending up here?" Wasting my time, effort, and maybe some emotions on a person who was not the best for me?

Nevertheless, God allowed me to realize that until I placed His standards as the first and most important priority in my life, I would continue to come up short. Once I understood that, I would have upfront conversations early on. I wouldn't beat around the bush about my desires and views to please God. I wouldn't hide my love for God for the next phone conversation or the next date. I wanted people to know the real me right away so that if it wasn't what they desired we could both protect ourselves.

One day, I was speaking to someone who appeared to be a stand up person, kind, thoughtful, charming, all these things that most women would want. I felt I needed to tell him about my desire to wait until marriage to have sex, so I did. At that point, it was no longer a choice but more like a must. Once I told him, he seemed to need more clarity.

Finally, he understood what I meant, and he nicely responded that I was a great girl but he could not remain faithful in a relationship with someone he could not have sex with. That night, we stopped talking and honestly, I was happy about it. I knew my standard and my desire was right for me. I personally did not want anyone who could not be with me without sex. End of story.

It got easier and easier as I matured and was locked in my decision to not only honor God but to trust Him with the love He had for me. Not everyone agreed with my position. As a matter of fact, someone once told me I was completely selfish for expecting any man to spend money, time, and effort on me without sex. I quickly learned not to defend myself against people who were not even called to walk in my shoes or weren't in a position to understand. I also learned how to discern false beliefs.

My pastor would always say, "How will you know the heart of God if you don't know His

Word?" Don't allow your ignorance or lack of knowledge to do something that compromises God's will for your life. If you are uncertain and indecisive about something, seek wise counsel. I'm never opposed to wise counsel; it's biblical: "Where no counsel is, the people fall: but in the multitude of counselors there is safety" (Proverbs 11:14).

You should never run away from true counsel because you don't want "someone all up in your business." That's a prideful mentality. I know because it used to be me. I grew up very independent and self- reliant; I was the oldest of my siblings and was nine years older than my sister. Therefore, I had to learn many things on my own or if my mom taught me, I had to demonstrate it on my own. As a result, when I became a teen or a young adult, I despised asking for help. I saw it as a sign of weakness.

If I struggled in an area, I would try to fix it on my own. But I would learn that's not a wise or mature way to live. If you are struggling with a subject at school, you can fail in silence or you can ask for a tutor. If you are having challenges excelling in a specific area on the job, you can reach out to a manager for assistance or you can continue to underperform. In relationships, you can seek out a trusted person to spiritually counsel you and your partner in preparation for marriage and the growth of your relationship or you can fight and fuss your way behind closed doors all the way to a divorce. Which options yield the best results? Being humble and seeking counsel.

You can try to start a successful business if you want but your pride will keep you with 20 loyal customers. You will not attain an international company with a spirit of pride because you don't want anyone telling you how to "run your business." Sit there and fiddle your way through if you like but know that greatness is followed by humility.

God has placed many people in our paths to help us navigate through life but what I find is lack of trust, shame, and pride keep many people from getting proper guidance. People will repeat cycles, fall time after time, get hurt repeatedly and deal with their problems alone instead of asking for help. Many times, we avoid accountability and responsibility for our actions.

Maybe if you talked to someone about your relationships, they could help you see that you have a problem with cutting people off. Maybe you lack compassion in certain areas so you feel there is no one out there for you when in reality you just have not grasped the idea of unconditional love.

Thankfully, our God knows what we can handle and when we can handle it. He will allow us to mature, develop and even encounter people who will show us proper standards. When we are complete in Him, He will allow certain things to come into our lives that He knows we can handle. His protection is truly priceless and is more valuable than we can ever understand.

 I want to admonish you to seek God's truth about His love for you as His child. Not what someone has told you, but from your experience. Get to know His unchangeable love for yourself. That comes through prayer and the Word. How will you know you are being taught the truth? If it lines up with the Word of God and Scripture. You can't only assume because you grew up in a church or that the old clichés or family sayings you have heard are the absolute truth. Hold them up to the true standard of God's Word. That way, you can walk in confidence and be sure of God's love for you and His forgiveness. Once you are secure in God's love, you will know how to extend love, compassion, and forgiveness to others. You will also display that same type of protection to the love God places in your life. It all starts and ends with Him.

Chapter 2

HIDDEN AND SET APART

"There has never been another you. With no effort on your part you were born to be something very special and set apart. What you are going to do in appreciation of that gift is a decision only you can make" - Dan Zadra

Living in this generation and being a true follower of Christ will cause you to be misunderstood because you are called to be set apart. The truth is not everyone will agree with the life you have chosen and might I add: it won't always be easy. When I first decided to seriously dedicate my life to God, I was about 18 years old. I instantly lost a few friends because of my zeal for God.

My desire to do things differently became unappealing to that group of people. I remember an old friend of mine sending me a long message about how she felt I was becoming too holy and judgmental for not wanting to go to parties. In all honesty, I was still struggling internally but I knew my life needed to go in a different direction. I tossed back and forth knowing I would lose that set of friends because it was clear the life I wanted was not the life they were interested in. I loved them very much but I loved God more. I learned later on that anyone God appoints to be on this journey with me will flow.

Now, make no mistake about it; it will require work, commitment, understanding, and forgiveness but overall, people who are God-ordained in your life will never make you choose between God's ways and theirs. Rather, they will aim to live His way too.

Not everyone will be as committed as you are to the principles of your faith. They will not understand why you tithe, why you give offerings each time you go to church, why you serve or volunteer at your local assembly and so forth. That is OK – everything just isn't meant to be understood by everyone.

    When I was single, people would ask me all the time why I was not in a relationship, why I was not going out to find love and why I wanted to abstain from certain activities and environments. Was it because I thought I was better than anyone else who was doing those things? Not in the least. I was tired of doing those things and ending up with no results in my life. Every time the thought crossed my mind to go back to my former ways, I remembered where I would always end up and it simply was not worth it for me. I actually got used to being misunderstood many times.

However, God sent some key people into my life who just "got me." It was so refreshing to be around individuals who understood my walk, my desire to please God and my way of thinking. With those people, I can be transparent, vulnerable, and draw strength from the connection. I don't have to drain, prove, or over-explain myself.

I have a friend right now who is a key part of my life and where I am currently. We can go weeks without talking but when we do connect, it's like we are right back on track. Some things we tell each other do not need to be fully explained because she knows me not only naturally but our spirits are familiar. At times, I am led to pray for her and after we converse, she would tell me something she was facing that confirmed what I prayed about. I like to call that intentional and divine connection. It's amazing how one person can see your ways as foreign data but another can be on the same page with you.

A Different Standard to Live By

I want you to know that if you are chosen by God and hidden in His will, the world will not understand many things about you because you are a part of the kingdom of God, which operates by a completely different standard. When I came to know Christ, I literally had to reprogram my thoughts, my ways of thinking about situations, my speech, my reactions – literally, everything had to be changed and is still being changed daily. The Word of God says in Romans 12:2, "Do not be conformed to the pattern of the world, but be transformed by the renewing of your mind. Then you will be able to test and approve what God's will is, his good pleasing and perfect will."

If you are constantly renewing your mind to think God's way, imagine the contrast between you and someone who is not even interested in knowing God's way. Pretty big difference. For example, God says love your neighbor as yourself and pray for your enemies. However, a person who has never heard that teaching will not understand why you would help a person who spoke badly about you or why you would not seek revenge when someone did you wrong.

Most people in the world's system believe in doing what feels right to them. If someone wrongs them, they will instantly retaliate. Imagine how much crime and death would be stopped if we all committed to changing our hearts to be like God's? Jesus Himself wasn't always understood or received by everyone. Still, that did not stop Him from fulfilling His assignment and coming down to earth, being betrayed, being hung on that cross, and rising to live again. He is our perfect model of someone who persevered in spite of.

As we go through life, our goal is not to be appealing to every single person on this earth but to be holy, acceptable, and pleasing to God our Father. The best thing about Him is that He sees and knows all. He understands the depths of our hearts. He knows our feelings before we reveal them to anyone else. He knows our hearts before we even pray. The Lord knows all the hidden secret things about us that we dare not tell another soul. He knows them and loves us just the same. It's simply mind-blowing to me.

Tamela Mann has a song called "Change Me" that touches my heart and does something different to me each time I hear it. I think about how far I've come and how much farther I need to go to be changed by God. I think about how my strength will never be enough. I remember the times I used to run from God after I did something I knew wasn't pleasing to Him. I would go days or weeks without praying because I felt I needed to wait until I got myself back together before going to Him again. Little did I know my lack of prayer did not keep God from knowing what was in my heart anyway. Really, all I ended up doing was making life harder for me by running away. I was carrying the weight of my sins in my heart, trying to hide, feeling shameful and unworthy of God's love and presence. Had I confessed my sins and been honest with God, He would have taken that burden and those feelings of shame and replaced them with His love and care. Praying would have strengthened and helped me to understand that I didn't have to sin because I had a way of escape through God's great love.

Don't ever allow anyone's perception of you, the fact that you are not understood, or even your own thoughts of yourself keep you from the presence of God or communicating with Him. He longs for your heart, your soul, and your mind. He's waiting to comfort and love you like no one else can.

Many Christians incorrectly perceive that works alone make you worthy of God's love. Let me tell you the truth: you can pray all day, work all night, cross every "T" and dot every "I" but it will not change God's unconditional love for you. Am I saying you should do whatever you want, live any kind of foolish way and expect to inherit the earth? No! I'm not condoning a sinful lifestyle but I am saying that we are all sinners in need of a Savior; we are saved by grace. It becomes easier to please God and have a desire to obey Him when we understand He loves us unconditionally, not based on performance. It will also help us to love others in that same light.

The Word of God says, "For a righteous man fall seven times and rise again, but the wicked shall fall by calamity" (Proverbs 24:16). So it's important that when you fall into temptation and sin that you repent and turn from your ways. Receive the grace and forgiveness of God. The

Enemy would love nothing more than for you to be bound by guilt and shame but that is not the will of God for you. Walk in your victory and allow God to continue to mold and shape you into what He has called you to be.

Chapter 3

LIVING ABOVE FEAR

"Have I not commanded you? Be strong and courageous. Do not be afraid; do not be discouraged, for the Lord your God will be with you wherever you go"(Joshua 1:9).

If we are going to walk in the complete fullness of God and His promises, part of the refining process is learning to live above fear. I could write an entire book on this topic alone because I feel it is the one emotion birthed by the Enemy that is so prevalent in the believer's life. We tackle so many of the obvious negative emotions: hatred, envy, malice, gossip, etc. However, fear is something that so many of us try to hide behind and justify. I've done it plenty of times in my life. It's a daily process to dismiss fearful living, a fearful mindset, and fearful actions. The Bible addresses fear over 30 times in many different situations; yet, it's something that we allow to control our lives.

Fear is birthed from many things but I can say that none of it is a gift or characteristic of God. For the Word of God says, "God has not given us the spirit of fear, but of power, love, and a sound mind" (2 Timothy 1:7). It is never God's will for us to be fearful of anything, no matter what reason we have or what justification we try to hold onto in our minds.

Fear has a crippling hold on our lives and robs us of many promises and wonderful experiences God wants for us. For example, there was a time in my life I was afraid to love or trust anyone because of a past experience that left me hurt. I feared that if I was vulnerable to another person, I would end up hurt and disappointed again. So as a defense, I made several statements in an attempt to justify my fears: "No one is truly honest. You can never really trust anyone these days. Don't put anything past anybody because you just never know."

So, just from my mindset, I was limiting my own life and sabotaging my own connections due to my pre-set way of thinking. I had to learn that if I was going to trust God with my heart, I had to let go of the fear of being hurt. I had to use wisdom to determine who I allowed to be close to me but it was unfair to others and my own future to believe that no one could be trusted. Distrust breeds more distrust and that cycle between two people just continues. I had to stop it.

Fear will also make you think or talk yourself out of a promise. The Bible says, "The tongue can bring death or life, those who love to talk will reap the consequences" (Proverbs 18:21). This principle is straightforward, and I can say that I have been guilty of speaking the wrong words over my life by negative talk about myself, my situation or anything pertaining to me. We can literally talk ourselves out of blessings because we allow fear to make us say things that are not in alignment with God.

If we want or believe that God will do something for us, we need to settle within our hearts that if it is in His will, He will do whatever we ask and pray for. We can't say one minute, "God I know you are able to do this" and later that day say, "It's probably not even going to work out" or "I'm not even going to get my hopes up."

Why not? God wants your hopes to be all the way to the roof with Him!

You cannot decide to stick with something without wavering because of what it looks like or because of the circumstances you face. Your mind has to be fixed. Period. No wavering allowed! One day, you will have to believe in a life or death situation and your faith will make all the difference.

Desperate Times Call for Extreme Faith

I want to share a very personal testimony about my life and a situation that I had to face that by far was the most intense I have had to deal with. I feel people everywhere need to know that God can do exceeding abundantly above all.

There was a time that my mom was gone for four days and could not be found. My mom is in her late 50's; however, she has had challenges with her memory but we believe God is a healer and a deliverer. The fact remains that she takes medicine to help improve her cognitive abilities. Throughout those four days, my faith was challenged. Her absence was detrimental to my faith and my life with God.

Fear tried to take over me telling me that we would never find my mother. The Enemy tried to set scenarios, thoughts, images, and all types of emotions to make me believe I would not see my mom alive again but I refused to receive them. I contacted some close people of strong faith to pray and stand in agreement with me during that time. Contacting the authorities and filing a missing person's report was a daunting task. I had to keep

my mind fixed on my mother being back home. I decided I could spend all my time focusing on the fear or kick my faith into full gear and believe God.

Looking back, I can't believe I was able to sleep those three nights that my mom was gone because humanly it shouldn't have been possible. Although I was afraid and concerned, I kept fighting the spirit of worry. I kept seeking the Holy Spirit in prayer and praise, thanking God for all things, and combating the emotions that were bombarding me.

The second day, I stayed home from work, took action to locate my mom, prayed and searched. I remember one particular day when fear overcame me, and I began to cry hysterically. I felt condemned for so many reasons (none of which were valid), and I was about to be all wrapped in my emotions. Thankfully, those close to me quickly spoke life into me and came against all those thoughts I felt because fear had planted false seeds of hopelessness in me.

God Will Reveal the End in the Middle of the Fight

I remember that day going back home and being so physically exhausted that I took a nap on the couch. During that nap, I had a dream I was on the phone with someone and my mom was standing in the doorway. The cry that I let out in the dream was so vivid, so real, and so strong. When I woke up from that nap, I knew that God had spoken to me through that dream; I was confident it wasn't something I dreamt out of thin air. I truly believe it was a prophetic dream that would show me what was to come. Right then, my faith was renewed to continue believing God for the victory.

The third day, I continued on. I still don't fully understand how God's strength allowed me to work a full day at my job not knowing exactly where my mom was. I remember fasting that day being very spiritually focused and strong. I refused to let my emotions get a hold of me. I would not allow guilt to tell me I should be out searching and crying to find her. I had done that and literally, all I had left to do was rest and believe God. Now, I know many people would think, "You can believe God all day but you have to take action; you have to do something Kamisha!" I definitely did all that was in my physical power to do including contacting the local news stations, corresponding with detectives in the city, even putting up missing person signs in my town. I did it all as I was led by the Holy Spirit. I didn't want to do anything that could worsen the situation.

I learned in that time of desperation that our hope has to be so fixed on God that nothing else matters. This doesn't make sense to some people who may not trust in the power of God or the power of prayer. People who rationalize their way through life have to use logic and reasoning. Faith does the complete opposite. I am constantly reminded of what Jesus said to the disciples: "With man this is impossible, but with God all things are possible" (Mathew 19:26).

Discernment and Wisdom

I was sitting at work one day and was tempted to go on my social media pages to share my mom's missing person report the news stations had sent me. Two major news stations had posted my mom on television and on their social media pages. Before going on social media, I told someone close to me what I was thinking and they replied, "If that is the direction God is leading you in then do it."

Well, I immediately felt convicted because God had not led me to do that. Did it seem like the logical and practical thing to do? Yea sure, tell as many people as you can so they can "help" you find her. The more people who know, the better the chances of getting her back home safely right? Not really.

Although I've lived in my current city for about a year and a half, not many people on my social networks live in this area. I am connected to a few co-workers but not really any friends, neighbors or people who could have gotten the information and help me locate my mom. I knew she was not out of state or out of town so using that method was not wise. One wrong move could have produced negative results.

That day, I learned how vital it is to use wisdom in all things. You can't rely on your thoughts and beliefs in the heat of a battle. One wrong move could cost you more than you planned. Later that day while I was at work, I spoke to a customer whom I had met for the first time. He said he had no idea what I was facing at that time but that God was going to birth ministry in me through my life journey.

He proceeded to tell me God was going to reveal things to me in dreams and take me to another level spiritually. He also encouraged me to keep holding on and trusting God because there is a great reward for me. Moreover, he imparted some godly wisdom about marriage and how his 25-year godly marriage was still going strong. Little did I know I would be engaged one month later.

As he talked to me, God was confirming his words in my spirit. He spoke very clearly, sharply, and directly. Once he was done, he didn't linger; he didn't try to have a personal conversation about me or my life. He just said, "divine appointments." That was another testament within this four-day testimony that really proved to me God was with me in my darkest moments.

Time Doesn't Change the Promise

That night would have completed the fourth day my mom had been missing without a trace. The detective who was communicating with me kept calling to check on me and to update and inform me of what they had done to locate my mom but there was still no trail. By that time, my emotions were at their worst because I was focused on how much time had passed since the last time I saw my mother. I kept thinking to myself, "It's going on four days; it's been too long." The Enemy tried to

tell me my mom was gone; that something tragic had taken place and that she was no longer alive. How crazy it is that those thoughts just came into my mind and caused me to believe them! But that's

just what fear is – False Evidence Appearing Real.

Nevertheless, I was reminded that as a believer, I have the power over the Enemy to trust God no matter what my situation looks like. In the refinery, you can't focus on the amount of time that has passed. You cannot allow the days, the months, or even the years make you waver on God's Word for your life. In such a critical situation, a person would say, "Timing is everything" and that is true to an extent. Yet, God's timing is not our timing and His ways are not ours.

You can stand on the Word of God that declares, "God is our refuge and strength, a very present help in trouble" (Psalm 46:1). He's never distant when it comes to your dependency on Him. He may be silent and He may allow you to experience apparently bad situations but just remember – it's working for your good.

As I lay in my mom's bed that night, I read John 11, which is the story about God raising Lazarus from the tomb after four days. I do not believe any of that night's events happened by chance. Rather, it was all intentional and a part of God's orchestration. Why is that? One, I have heard the story of Lazarus many times in church so I knew it. However, that day was the first time I had read the entire story for myself in my private time. Two, I was at a pivotal time in my life when I clung to this word like my next breath depended on it because it seriously did!

Negative thoughts tried to consume my mind but I'm so thankful I could discern they were not of God. As a result, I did not receive or dwell on them but I did have to work to fight against them.

Faith Partners: Iron Sharpens Iron

I called up a very close friend of mine and explained to her what was happening. Immediately, she prayed and placed confidence in God to bring my mother home quickly. She said, "This is not going to be a long and drawn out work but she is going to be found today or tomorrow, at the latest."

I'm so glad to have faith partners in my life who know what to pray and how to reach heaven; such relationships are priceless. If you do not have friends or anyone in your life like this I suggest you pray and ask God to open your heart and mind to receive these types of people. I strongly believe God did not place us on the earth to be isolated from other believers; we do so on our own. The very Word of God says, "Iron sharpens iron, so a friend sharpens a friend" (Proverbs 27:17).

It is true that during this challenging time, my friend's faith built me up. Her level of belief sharpened and helped drive the fear out of me. I had two other close friends who did the same. One of them prayed saying that whoever my mom came into contact with would be gracious and kind to her wherever she was. I did not have the kind of prayer within me but I do believe the Holy Spirit used her to pray so accurately over my mother's life.

The next day, I went to work feeling ten times better. No longer was I moved by the amount of time that had passed or by the state of my emotions. I was not afraid or weary; my soul was just confident and I trusted in God's plan that much. My phone rang around 9:30 AM, it was a sheriff calling to tell me that he had found my mother and she was safe and sound. Immediately, I bent over and let out the same cry that I did when I had the dream of finding my mom just two days prior. Every bit of doubt, fear, unbelief, grief, worry, and anything else that the Enemy tried to plant in my mind had been defeated! God had won the victory once again.

I learned endless lessons about fear in those four days. Fear really tried to bombard my mind, feed me lies, make me believe things that weren't true and convinced me to give in to a reality that wasn't even there. Was I perfect in the battle? Not at all. I took many blows, had an emotional breakdown for about 30 minutes and a crying spell another day. However, one thing I can say is I refused to let fear win over me. Each time I felt it trying to overtake me, I chose to believe God instead. I kept holding on to the fact that I knew the feelings did not come from God. Although He was with me during every stage of the situation, those negative thoughts were not of Him. I was His child so I chose to follow what *my* Father told me, not the father of lies, Satan.

Today, my mom is doing well; she is excellent and amazing. She was divinely covered by God for those four days. God did not allow any hurt, harm or danger to come to her body. She could have been destroyed in the state she was in – but God! Just as my friend had prayed, someone did come in contact with her and was very helpful and gracious to her. The person was able to take the proper steps to get her back home! The prayers of the righteous do avail and faith really does change things!

You have the power to decide that you will not allow fear to control you or even cause you to be stagnant in your life. Fear does not always manifest itself in the big things like jumping out of a plane or in a huge natural disaster. The main type of fear that keeps the average person down is the fear of small things. It comes in the form of not being open to new people, not wanting to trust others because you were hurt by someone in a relationship, a friendship or by a family or church member.

Many people have been sexually abused by those they trusted or were close to and it created emotional blockages in their lives. Others have experienced betrayal in the church and although they may still attend church, they distance themselves or place a wall between them and others.

You might feel people are out to sabotage you so you don't want anyone around that you aren't forced to deal with. Trust me, I know all those feelings but fear is not worth giving into. I look back on my life and recall how my mom would make me face the things I was afraid of for me to conquer that fear.

I encourage you to do the same. Face the very things in you that keep you from moving forward to the next level. Apply for that job you've been thinking about. Take that class that you have been putting off. Start that workout plan. Go to that meeting that you always make an excuse not to attend and live! Life is not meant to spend hiding in the shadows of fear, doubt, and worry. The Holy Spirit empowers us to do all things with God's power and strength. Choose today to go forward with power and boldness. You are not too young or too old to make those type of changes in your life, your future self will reap that harvest of the fearless life you live today!

Chapter 4

ELIMINATING DISTRACTIONS

"Don't let the things of the world distract you. Focus on your purpose" – **Sunday Adelaja**

Being aware of distractions is one of the most powerful tools we can learn to use in our lives. Many dreams are deferred, destiny's cut short, and people have just thrown in the towel because of this one word – "distractions." Distractions are designed to creep in, divert your focus, and change your course – if you allow it. The word "distraction" is defined as a thing that prevents someone from giving full attention to something else. Another definition is extreme agitation of the mind or emotions.

Being distracted in life can be very costly. Many times in my life, I allowed distractions to set me off track but I am thankful I have the power to overcome them when I submit to God's will for me. You may have decided that you are going to live for God, walk in His way, treat others with love, pray for your enemies, and do everything that the Word of God requires of you. Your intentions are pure and your motives are genuine. You are off to a great start and walking on a wonderful path.

However, you must be aware that the Enemy neither wants you to fulfill anything God set out for you nor does he want you to inherit any of the promises of God. He will set up distractions in your heart, your mind, your day, and in any way he can to throw curveballs at you.

Below you will read about a few types of distractions that will come your way, how you can be aware of them and how to keep focused on God to stay in His will.

Emotional Distractions

Our feelings are the one thing we are not aware of sometimes that can keep us from doing what we are called to do. They can keep us bound and living very limited lives if we are not careful. We are called to live by faith, not by our feelings. The Bible speaks about matters of the heart and why we shouldn't allow our feelings to control us. Proverbs 3:5-6 says: "Trust in the Lord with all your heart, and do not lean to your own understanding. In all your ways acknowledge him, and he will make your path straight."

This tells us that our understanding of life is not as accurate as God's. He also tells us that His thoughts are not our thoughts and His ways are not our ways. The more dependent we are on Him, the better off we will be. It all goes back to how much we trust Him and what His Word has to say. Some emotions that can creep in our lives to distract us are worry, fear, anxiety, doubt, anger, jealousy, envy, insecurity, confusion, and the list continues. Not one of these feelings is the will of God for the believer's life. They come to separate us from God's peace and comfort. They create a space between us and our goals. They distort our vision and if we don't ever recognize them, they can leave us stagnant for years. Once your vision is distorted, everything is altered.

As I'm writing this chapter today, I'm overcoming a challenge with my left eye. For the past few days, my eyes have been extremely dry. They suddenly turned red and a few days ago, vision in one of my eyes became blurry. I'm not an eye doctor so the first thing I did was pray for my sight to be properly restored. Then, I set an urgent appointment with my optometrist.

The blurriness in that one eye is a distraction to me at the present time. The first day or so when I noticed the change I did what many of us do, I went online to Google and typed in "blurriness in one eye." All types of things came up that could be the cause – some minor, and some major including cataracts, which is a serious eye disease that can cause blindness. Of course, when I read that, fear tried to creep in, especially because during my last eye exam, I chose not to have dilation in my eyes. Eye dilation allows the optometrist to see deeper into your eye and detect any possible issues that could be arising.

The thought came to my mind that something more could be wrong. I immediately shut that thought down, guarded my mind and stopped the computer searches. I decided I would claim healing for my eye, go to my doctor and get the proper examination. See how quickly that could have gone left? If I had allowed it to, I could have spoken all types of things and created a false scenario in my mind just because of a distraction I allowed.

When I actually saw my doctor, he did some eye tests and told me my eyes were severely dry but I had no serious issues and no cataracts. He gave me a medicated eye drop prescription to use, and I went about my day. I wonder what would have happened if I had chosen to dwell on the negative possibilities – conjuring up all types of scenarios that were not even true.

I feel that many of us unintentionally do that in our lives. We let insecurities speak to us and tell us we don't look good enough the way we are and that we aren't attractive because we don't look like people we see in the media. We allow fear to tell us that we shouldn't step out and do what we truly desire for a living. We listen to that voice that says we should continue to play it safe in a secure job that we don't even like. We let the world's system tell us that being sexy, vulgar, and ungodly will benefit us more than living lives of purity. Unfortunately, we become focused on what we see around us rather than what we believe.

Distractions in Your Heart: You Can't Be Led by Feelings

When it comes to our hearts, we get hurt often because we grow up hearing the many clichés from the age of Disney that say, "Follow your heart." Moreover, there are many other songs, movies, and messages that tell us to do what we feel. We fall into this whirlwind of emotions and think it's perfectly OK when it starts off favorably. However, when the emotions flip, we make our choices based on those unfavorable emotions and "follow our hearts." Subsequently, we back out of the situation without a second thought.

My heart has steered me in the wrong direction many times in life. After making many unwise choices, I decided to let God lead me. I learned that the Spirit will always reveal the truth and show you the things to come; on the other hand, the heart will deceive you. "The heart is deceitful above all things and beyond cure. Who can understand it?" (Jeremiah 17: 9).

Many times, I get wrapped up in my feelings; they control how I think, and act. In those moments, I have to stop and realize that my feelings are temporary. Therefore, being emotionally led is one of the worst habits we can form as believers.

Our feelings can change about 20 times or more a day depending on the events in that day. Today's society is easily led by feelings and emotions resulting in divorce rates soaring higher than ever; more families are broken. People are not sticking to their goals because emotional distractions will cause you to forfeit your original plans.

We must learn that feelings are temporary but God's plans remain the same. If we break a covenant based on an emotional feeling, it means we do not understand the value of commitment, perseverance, longsuffering, and unconditional love. When Jesus went to the cross, it wasn't because He felt like dying for our sins. He knew it was the will of the Father for Him. While He was beaten, whipped, and had nails pierced in His hands, He could have allowed His emotions to make Him curse God to His face. Jesus could have said any and everything. Yet, through it all, He remained loyal and committed to carrying out God's will so that we could be set free.

I am very thankful that God is the greatest example of love, commitment, covenant, patience, and longsuffering. I challenge you to seek Him concerning your feelings and emotions. Give your feelings to Him in exchange for His peace, His love and rest, which He has made available to you.

Choose today that you will no longer allow emotional distractions to dictate to your life, your decisions, and your destiny. We become mature followers of Jesus when we learn how to shut down feelings that are not of God and claim dominion and victory over our flesh being led by the Holy Spirit. Set your heart and mind on things eternal, and you will never be steered on the wrong path.

Social Distractions: The New Age Communication

This one is huge and is also so prevalent today. It's a form of distraction that is harder to tame. Why? Well, if you're anything like me and you love people, it can be hard to discipline yourself in this area. You want to be constantly present in people's lives to encourage, guide or be a listening ear. Other times, you may just truly enjoy the company of being around certain people. As good as that may be, you can slowly become dependent, needing to always do something or say something.

At times, we need to become content with spending time with God in silence or focusing on a specific assignment without trying to spread ourselves thin. I learned a few years ago that my quality of life and productivity were not based on how many Christian events I could attend, how many church programs I could make it to or how much I could be in on something that's happening.

For about two years, I was very intentional with God so He could direct my path the way He wanted it to go. During those two years, I seldom watched television. I remember having one but never really looked at it much. I did still watch movies when something good was showing but I didn't have that commitment to catch up on what was on.

Prior to that, I was heavily engaged in such things so I believe God took away those desires so He could impart His divine wisdom, knowledge, and power into me. After work, if I didn't have church that night, I would go to Barnes and Nobles Book Store and read my Bible or books that I saw there. That was also in the beginning stages of my writing when I would blog and create content.

I would also be very intentional about my interactions on social media. I remember scrolling through my timeline some days just being so discouraged and turned off by some of the negative things I would see. My social networks were filled with all types of fighting videos, vulgarity and profanity. It affected me so seriously that I didn't want to log on.

One day, a friend told me something profound: "Your social networks are a reflection of what you allow and what you attract." What? No, it was not! I argued that for so long. I said that I don't have control over what these people do and say so how can I change what I see?

I began to filter what was coming through and looked at my lists and networks only to find that many of the people weren't a significant part of my life. I had added people over the years from school, parties I used to attend, organizations I knew of or just being nice and accepting random requests from those with no commonalities. Now, I am not saying I was too good to be connected to such people but if I wanted to change what I was seeing, I had to readjust what I allowed into my eyes and my ears. I ended up shutting my social media accounts completely down in 2013 and starting new accounts. This time, I was more purposeful about who I added to my social space. I would take a second to actually see if I knew someone before just clicking a button to expose myself to them.

We have to learn to value ourselves more than feeling the need to be validated or known by everyone. You are not for everyone and everyone will not be for you; that is going to be completely fine at the end of the day. I can truly say that my social networks are full of inspiring, funny, amazing individuals. I can look at each contact and know why I have that person on my network even if I might not have met him or her personally.

If God is to control every aspect of our lives, we have to really turn everything over to Him. Let

Him do a total makeover on those areas that can be hindrances. At times, we need to put down our phones and place them on "Do not disturb" for a day. That way, we will not be socially distracted by the apps, the notifications, the DM's, and all other types of deterrents.

How great would it be if we took all those small minutes per day that we use to check our social media accounts, our emails, favorite apps, and just traded them in for moments of spiritual maintenance? Wouldn't it be more beneficial if we memorized a scripture, prayed for someone in need or spent that time thanking God for what He is doing in our lives? How much better off would we be? I know you might be thinking, "Kamisha, really? This all sounds so extra and unnecessary" but I challenge you to just try it. For one week, limit your exposure to being so socially distracted. Are you the type of person who just has to post something every day? Guess what. It will still be there when you return. The world will not stop! Just watch how much your heart and mind will have a chance to de-clutter by a week of change in that area.

As it is for me right now, I'm taking a step back from social media so I can focus on this assignment. I can continue to check my networks and post every day. Alternatively, I can zone in and focus on the call and assignment I know God has placed on my life and get it done.

God is very intentional; He is not a time waster so why would I not use the precious time He has given me to the best of my ability? Great things wait on the other side for those who obey God. I want to be on the winning side. You can too! Let God refine your social life. You may be developing a business; you may be an entrepreneur and so you feel social networking is the heart of what you do. Can I be honest with you? It's not the heart of what you do! God should be there. While the advancements of social media have made business and resources easily accessible, we don't have to rely on that for our sources. If you seek

God's face and His will with all your heart, He will cause all grace to abound toward you and have it all work out for your good.

Chapter 5

ADVERSITY TO YOUR ADVANTAGE

"You should never view your challenges as a disadvantage. Instead, it's important for you to understand that your experience facing and overcoming adversity is actually one of your biggest advantages" – Michelle Obama.

Your life challenges can do one or two things: they can help you develop into a stronger, better, wiser person, or they can break and shatter you. What makes the difference in your outcome? Having an understanding of adversity in your life. How your perspective of the challenges that may arise will shape if you sink or swim.

The first step to using adversity to your advantage is believing in the Word of God concerning tests and trials. Believe it or not many Christians will say they believe everything in the Word of God but don't bother to believe the parts that force them out of their comfort zones.

We believe that God is the God of grace, blessings, favor, "things," and He can make everything go our way. Yes, those things are easy to believe. However, we struggle with the part of the Bible that talks about suffering, enduring trials and tribulations, and not growing weary in well doing. It's all in there. James 1:2-5 says, "Consider it pure joy, my brothers and sisters, whenever you face trials of many kinds, because you now that the testing of your faith produces perseverance. Let perseverance finish its work so that you may be mature and complete, not lacking anything."

Perception of the Process: Your Eyes Matter

Your perception of what happens in your life plays a major role in your seasons of refining. Many people are stuck in a rut because they constantly avoid change; they run from any type of discomfort or stretching. To be honest, if you are a person who cannot perceive challenge as a catalyst for greater, you will be very limited. For example, when a couple decides they want to have children, they must count all the costs. Children are blessings and an inheritance from the Lord. Their conception, creation, and purpose are for the good of anyone who is blessed to have them.

It is an honor to be a parent, to raise children, train them in the way they should go and aid them to their destinies. However, the process of doing so will come with its share of tests and trials, even times that are plain hard. It doesn't mean that the couple should back out of having children. Rather, it means they should get a proper expectation of the job at hand.

Making a child is a process that requires a man and a woman coming together to create the child in the mother's womb. From the point of conception, the process begins. The woman's body begins to go through changes physically; she may even experience emotional and hormonal changes throughout the pregnancy. Some pregnant women experience sickness, nausea, hair loss, fatigue, and many negative changes. On the other hand, some people experience major hair growth, no sickness, no major fatigue and do not have to face many emotional challenges. Everyone is different.

Labor is also different for every mother. I've talked to some women who had a very quick and easy labor while some spent more than 40 hours total in labor to birth their blessings. Although one hundred women will have different experiences in some way, most women will agree on one thing: pregnancy and childbirth were worth all the challenges, the pain, and the sacrifices they endured to bring their beautiful children into the world. It may be easy to picture and you might ask, "Who wouldn't see having a child as a great thing?" Well, again it's all about the perception of the moments of adversity.

Some couples pray for a child, then when the child comes, they become depressed; they lose sight of their vision because the new baby causes them to sleep less and their marriage "routine" is interrupted with greater challenges. They are faced with more responsibilities, and sometimes, instability in their schedules. Events that may take place with the new baby, demands on finances and needing the support of extended family more than before can all take a toll on the couple. Couples or new parents can become frustrated with themselves or each other and begin to even question if they made the right decision to have children when they did.

One spouse may shift blame on the other spouse who may have wanted children more than he/she did. Guess what? The blessing is still there. The honor of being a parent is still great; the privilege of caring for a gift from God is still very rewarding. But it's wrapped up in change, growth, and discomfort because it takes learning, patience, and a total surrender to God's plans to raise a child.

You can't be so in control of every penny, every minute of your day that you are not open to the pliability needed in this season. God wants to do something with new parents in the season of having a newborn.

Maybe a higher level of communication is needed to make things work better. Possibly a bit of selfishness that lingered in the marriage needs to be worked out so that parents are no longer blaming each other for challenges. Instead, they are learning to come together and lean on one another for comfort, encouragement, and strength.

Often times, having a child will mean spending less time with other couples than before because the focus is on your new addition. Every journey is different. We must be able to stand on the Word of God and know that adversity strengthens us.

This doesn't seem right: Sticking through the ugly phase of developing greatness

You cannot second guess your season due to the presence of adversity. Overcoming challenges is necessary to be prepared for your greater level of anointing. If you are single and praying for God to "send" your spouse, you should gear your prayers to being prepared for the responsibility, humility, and perseverance it takes to be in a relationship that is geared toward marriage.

    A lot of times in our generation, we see someone's end-result on social media, TV, or snippets of a couple's life, and we expect to just receive that product instantly. What we don't consider is that every strong marriage endured a detailed and extensive process of refining. It persevered through hard times, uncomfortable times, and seasons of trials and tribulations. Don't believe it to be true? Ask a godly couple who has a successful marriage. They will tell you how much forgiveness was required, how much grace, how much trust it took to get to the place that you are seeing. If we don't expect trials and don't prepare to get through them, we will faint, quit, and run when they come.

I remember when I first got into a relationship after being completely single for five years. I was hit with the reality that my single season was ending and my journey toward marriage had begun. I had to let go of my single ways of thinking and living. Although my single life was very focused on God, it was so much easier to manage my time because I only had to be accountable to me. I spent time with my family when I could but I was not obligated to "check in" when I got off work or let someone know I arrived at a place safely after traveling. The little things that one must consider when your life begins to merge with another person are crucial.

My relationship is a complete blessing, a divine gift and connection I believe God allowed to take place at the right time for me. However, during times of growth, if I fail to keep a proper perspective of it all, I could begin to complain. One time, out of sheer frustration, I found myself saying, "Life was so much easier when I was single." Immediately, I felt convicted. What that translated to was I was avoiding the season that caused me to grow and prepare to be a wife. Of course, life is "easier" when you don't have to work on your character anymore. I had become complacent with my ways.

As a single, no one reflects on your communication skills, your attitude and the things you do and say that need to be matured. Of course, life is "easier" without the need to level up but what would you rather have? A life of growth that is open and ready to receive God's promises or just a life of excuses and complacency? I quickly had to pray and ask God to change my perspective and help me to cherish and appreciate the growing pains that came with developing in my relationship. I asked Him to deliver me from that "flighty mentality" that wanted to run from things when they got difficult.

What I learned and saw with my own eyes is that with each hard conversation, each rough day I overcame, our relationship grew; I got closer to the man I would eventually marry. We became more stable, the love grew stronger, the security was there, the level of offense decreased, and we were building something solid.

There were days I just thanked God because I saw the fruit of our labor being manifested. I saw that each time we endured, we gained strength. My relationship was another vehicle that strengthened my trust and faith in God. I knew I could not tip-toe around trying to see if things would work out for my God but I had to begin to KNOW and rest assured that the entire process was working out for my God. I had to trust that God was with me every step of the way. He knew I would face the days I did but He had a perfect plan in the midst of it.

A morbidly obese person who starts to change his/her eating habits, exercises and goes to the gym will realize that things often get worse before they get better. The body has to adjust to a different lifestyle from the one it was used to for so long.

When the person stops drinking soda and a lot of sodium, they may experience headaches, stomach aches, and the body may react negatively at first. After the first week of going to the gym and executing their work out plans, they may feel worse than they did before they started. Why? It's a stage of growth that's interrupting that comfort zone. It was a dangerous, unhealthy zone but it was comfortable nonetheless. Many times, people quit before they can get to see any results because they couldn't endure that small period of opposition. If they had just kept going, being consistent and not stopping, they would have seen results and recognized that their choice to change was a great thing.

I want to encourage you to continue your process of growth. God has not left you although times may be hard and it may be difficult to endure. Your promotion will cost you days of discomfort. Learning that new program or having that greater responsibility will sometimes feel like it's out of your league. You may become frustrated and that's OK but don't second guess your blessing. If you are preparing for marriage and it seems like life is just different all around for you, that's great. You are developing into the spouse God is calling you to be. If you're becoming different from the person you were last year, don't fight the process. It's vital to be equipped for your next season.

We can't walk in greatness and be avoiders of challenges. Rather, we must learn to face and embrace them head on so we can get to the other side. God is with you each day; He will never leave you or forsake you. Stick with His plan and you will see His greater purpose for your life.

Chapter 6

WITHSTANDING FIRE

"Fire is the test of gold; adversity, of strong men" –

Martha Graham

For God's glory to truly be revealed in your life, He has to burn away some things so that only what reflects Him will be revealed. Would you take a piece of coal from a mine, place it on a necklace and present it to someone as a gift? Actually, the person would probably be insulted because they can't see the potential in the piece of coal and how it could be a beautiful shining diamond. That piece of coal has to go through something. It must withstand heat, fire, sawing, polishing, all the way down to a final inspection. Some things in your life will not make it through the refining process. The separation may be painful but at the end of the process, you will appreciate that God stripped away everything that was not fit for His use and for your destiny.

The time will come when certain people will not go with you to the next level. You may have had friends in your life for a particular season. Maybe you were in school and your classmates helped you persevere through your studies. You may have had some co-workers with whom you built some great ties for the season in your life, or perhaps, you had a relationship that came to teach you some lessons. Nevertheless, those people were not God-ordained to be your husband or your wife.

The key to being refined is staying surrendered to the move of God. Not becoming attached to things and people but staying committed to God's divine plan. This is where faith is truly tested and tried. A person who is committed to God's plan is confident and understands that if a relationship ends, it doesn't mean you will never get married, have children, or experience the love of a spouse. It just means that the promise will not be fulfilled alongside that person. If you get laid off from your job, and you think you won't be able to pay your bills; you won't stay ahead, and your life is about to go downhill, who do you really have trust in? The company you worked for or God? Who is the Author and Finisher of your faith?

It's amazing how we "church" week after week, attend service after service, but our trust and our hearts are in the hands of so many things other than God. We must realize that we have a responsibility to maintain our hope and trust in Him at all times, no matter what the circumstances are. We must become fire-proof.

I'm reminded of Daniel's process, and I encourage you to read it for yourself to gain even more understanding. Daniel was a very smart and intelligent man whom God granted favor with the king. One thing about Daniel that stood out was that he operated differently. He made up his mind to do the will of God no matter what others were doing. He wasn't a crowd follower but a Christ follower and a leader in his own right.

When he was chosen along with Hananiah, Shadrach, Meshach, and Abednego, he refused to be like the others who ate the royal food and drank all the wine. To avoid defiling his body, he asked to eat a vegetarian diet.

Let's talk about his discipline! I wonder, how many people would have chosen to take that route with the chance to eat any and everything in sight? Daniel was peculiar. He was on that Whole Foods meal plan!

The Bible says after ten days of eating veggies and only water, the men looked healthier and better nourished than any of the men who ate the royal food (Daniel 1:15). Right here, I learn that discipline and sacrifice yield greater results. The Bible goes on to say when they were presented to the King Nebuchadnezzar, he found no one equal to the men. In every area that the king questioned the men, he found them ten times better than all the magicians and enchanters in his entire kingdom!

Throughout Daniel's life, his different lifestyle brought him both challenges and calamities. But through it all, God allowed favor to fall on Daniel who had the gift of interpreting dreams, visions, and had lots of wisdom. At his request, he had the king appoint three men to his administration in the province of Babylon where they lived: Shadrach, Meshach, and Abednego.

The Heat of the Journey

King Nebuchadnezzar made an image of gold, which was very high and wide. It was set up in the city of Babylon where he lived. He commanded everyone in the town to gather around and participate in the dedication of the image. Then, he commanded all the people:

As soon as you hear the sound of the horn, flute, zither, lyre, harp, pipe, and all kinds of music, you must fall down and worship the image of gold that King Nebuchadnezzar set up. Whoever does not fall down and worship will immediately be thrown into a blazing furnace (Daniel 3:5-6 NIV).

During your process of greatness, you will be tested and tried to do things that go against God's will and challenge your integrity. These testings will reveal the core of your faithfulness. Sometimes, people who have authority over you will command you to do something that doesn't align with your morals, values, and beliefs. Have you ever been at work and was faced with a decision to honor God or do what was in the best interest of your job? Maybe a superior told you it was OK to do something that you know was not in line with the heart and mind of God. What do you do in such circumstances? My answer is simple: trust God. It won't be easy. You may get some or a great deal of persecution behind it but God has a way of avenging those who submit fully to Him.

The men refused to bow to the golden image of Nebuchadnezzar, and when confronted, they replied:

King Nebuchadnezzar, we do not need to defend ourselves before you in this matter. If we are thrown into the blazing furnace, the God we serve is able to deliver us from it, and he will deliver us from your Majesty's hand. But even if he does not, we want you to know, your Majesty, that we will not serve your gods or worship the image of gold you have set up (Daniel 3:16-18).

We will experience seasons where God will rock our boats, sink our ships, and wreck our worlds so we can learn to withstand the hardest times. Soon, we will learn that He is our world. Our savings accounts of 401k and our retirement plans are not what keep us afloat. God has all power in His hands concerning our lives.

I have met people who are so spiritually unaware of the wonders of God. They have never encountered God's Spirit or His mighty hand in a personal way. You can have a conversation with a person and discern if he /she has a personal relationship or encounter with God. People who have seen God do the miraculous are passionate; you can't shut them up about what God has done for them. When people try to come up with scientific data, limitations, or statistics about a particular subject, the person who has seen God do the impossible will always let that be his or her driving force.

The process of refinement wipes away doubts, insecurities and any questions that God is real because there is a point where you are left with nothing else to rely on but Him. When you are placed in the refinery, doubt melts, selfishness melts, self-righteousness burns away; pride is dismantled, and resentment is washed away. In the refinery, God has you so focused on Him that every waking moment is dependent on His presence in your life.

God Will Avenge

Once the three men refused to worship the image, the king became angry. The Bible says his attitude changed. He ordered the furnace to be heated seven times hotter than normal and then had some of the strongest soldiers tie the men up and thrown into the furnace. They were wearing their robes, trousers, turbans and other clothes.

Check this out: the king was very angry and ordered everything to be done so quickly that the flames killed the soldiers who took the men to the furnace! Now, that is some crazy type of heat. Guess what? It still was not enough to destroy the ones whose faith stood firm in the power of God. Once in the fire, someone reported to the king that there were no longer three but four men in the furnace. Not only was it simply amazing that one person got inside the furnace with them but they were now freely walking around where they got thrown in with their hands and feet tied!

Untouched by Flames: Your Enemy Cannot Destroy You

Nebuchadnezzar was so shocked he called on the men to come out of the furnace. All the important people: the government leaders, king's counselors, came around to see for themselves how this mighty miracle had taken place. The fire had not touched them; not one single hair on their heads was singed or scorched. Not one mark was on their clothes, not even the smell of fire was on them! My God! You really have to understand that this could only have been done by the hand of God being on their lives and supernaturally covering them. God can do the same great acts in your life! In fact, I want you to think right now about some situations you know you deserved an outcome of destruction in – but God!

No matter how long you have been saved, you have sinned against God; you have fallen short. If you're human like me, you've sometimes created your own mess; yet, God still did not allow you to be put to shame, be publicly humiliated, embarrassed or exposed. No! You don't look like many of the things you've been through; you don't smell like the messes that you've made. God's glory has covered you and shined over your life so people have no idea some of the internal thoughts you've overcome, the private victories you've won or the secret issues that He has delivered you from! God has a way of getting into these areas of your life and making you fireproof. Only His likeness and His glory can make it out!

Your Fire Produces His Glory

When I endured the most desperate times in my life, I realized God was birthing a beautiful thing inside of me. He was developing a new level of faith, a greater dependency, a stronger passion, uprooting religion and establishing His supernatural power in my life. The things I have seen in my life have made me unable to ever be kept in a religious box.

I believe that is what God wants to do for all His children in the kingdom of God. He wants to use your moments of fire and refinement to bring out something great inside of you. He wants to take your moments of, "I don't know what to do anymore" and empower you with His wisdom. He wants to make you vulnerable to Him so you can no longer care about what people think of you. You will soon learn that the people you try to captivate cannot do half of what God can do for you. We try to impress people in our lives, at work, church, our peers, and whoever else we come in contact with on a daily basis. Guess what? The biggest disappointment you will face is placing your hope and trust in humans only to find when you're in the fire, very few people will stand in it with you. That's why the Word of God says "Trust in the Lord with all thine heart and lean not unto your own understanding, in all your ways acknowledge him and he will make your path straight" (Proverbs 3:5).

Trust in God is Strengthened in Heated Battles
You can't live your life to the glory of God unless you learn to trust Him with all of your heart, mind, and soul. That means there is nothing left for you to place in the hands of man. Even when you have

earthly love in your life whether it is family, friends or even a spouse, it is healthy to trust them but not place all your trust in them. So when they fall short or disappoint you, you can live through the experience because your expectations of them are not unrealistic. We can't expect people to act as God in our lives but we can trust the God in them. We must learn how to withstand hard times when it comes to relationships as well.

If we lack commitment, tolerance, and understanding and then say that no one in our lives is worthy of our love that's not the right perspective. No, bro or sis – love suffers long, it endures, and it perseveres. It seeks to love from the inside out just as God does.

Understanding the Qualities in Others

I remember when I was living in sin that God had patience with me; grace and mercy followed me and as God began to change me, He dealt with every part of my heart from the inside out. He worked on my upbringing, my childhood, my teenage years, everything I lacked growing up and every bit of ignorance I had in me due to lack of knowledge. He dealt with it all and is still to this day reshaping me into a better woman.

When I prayed the prayer of salvation and got saved, my process of "living right" was not instant. Our understanding of who the people are in our lives won't happen right away and being able to communicate with people properly won't always come easily. But God will use certain people in our lives to develop character within us. We cannot run from the opportunities to become better by learning to love others.

Perhaps, you may be a very opinionated person with a strong personality. You may not understand others who are more introverted and less vocal. I know several years ago, I used to be frustrated around friends who were super timid and wouldn't speak their minds the way I did. I hated seeing people get "taken advantage of" and could not understand why people would remain quiet when they should speak up for themselves. Little did I know, I didn't have the godly wisdom to see the high value in those types of people.

Through a long process, God has made me more like the people I speak of. Thank God, I'm not the person who always has to speak her mind anymore. Let me just be completely honest, my opinionated personality is a strength but has also been an area of opportunity for me. It's something God has been helping me to balance.

Lately, I've also learned I don't have to try to defend myself when someone says or does something wrong against me. I have learned to take my concerns to God in prayer. I am still very articulate, educated, and smart. However, now, I am wise and I know that there is a way to express oneself without being out of line.

Sometimes, we don't like qualities in others because they intimidate or challenge us in some way. I understand now that challenge is good. We can't resist or run from certain connections because we don't immediately "gel" with someone. If God placed you with people who were just like you, how would you grow? How would you learn to adapt to different personalities? How would you learn to have your views and be strong about them if they were never challenged?

For those who are called to serve in the area of business or to be business owners, you must learn to love people of all types. You have to learn how to communicate with people unlike your family members, church members, classmates, and close friends. There is more in store for you when it comes to the development of your character and ability to impact people from different backgrounds. The key is allowing God to place you in that season or situation of fire so you can come out better and brighter.

Patience with Others and Their Process

I remember years ago having a co-worker who came to work each day complaining about her home life. She was in a verbally and emotionally abusive relationship and her overall outlook on life was very pessimistic. To be completely honest, it irritated me to work so close to her every day. I would come to work on such a high positive note about my day and within 20 minutes, she would make a negative comment about the job, the night she had or one of our supervisors. Something was always wrong.

After a while, as she continued to share her life stories with me, I began to realize that she just didn't have anyone to talk to about her situation. I began to pray for her outside of work but my prayers were selfishly motivated as I asked God to stop her from talking to me! God convicted me and showed me how selfish I actually was.

If I'm a true believer of the gospel and the good news of Jesus Christ, I should be using those opportunities as times to encourage her, build her faith and share the Word of God with her. After all, she was coming to me daily, and I was providing no answers because I was too busy being selfish and annoyed.

Once I realized God had placed me in that situation to be a light, things soon began to change. I would listen to her, then, I would just share some friendly advice. I wasn't preaching or pulling out a Bible but I was sharing the Word in conversation telling her she was worth much more than she was accepting.

Over the course of a few months, she was talking differently; she wasn't complaining as much (not around me, at least). She would come to work on Mondays and say "I thought about what you told me this weekend, and I didn't go there like

I used to." I was truly touched by that season with her because I realized what an amazing person she was on the inside. She was kind, loving, and just wanted someone to listen to her; she was searching for love. As a result, she was always pouring her heart out to the wrong people who ended up hurting her. She began to see more of her value and worth because someone was telling her daily that she was enough; she was worth it, and she was not crazy because of her desire to end a toxic lifestyle.

I won't ever forget that time in my life because it not only helped me shine light to someone else, but it helped me more than I ever imagined. These days, when I encounter people who have imperfections just as I do, it reminds me of God's great love for me. It's very hard for me to cast people out because of their shortcomings because I'm always reminded of mine. I remember how guarded I used to be, how disrespectful I was with my mouth using words as a defense mechanism for my hurt.

God had to burn and strip away so many layers of me in the fire to make me more loving, more compassionate, more tolerant and more sensitive to the hearts of others. I also know that being refined will be an ongoing process.

There are times even now when I fall short. I say and do things in ways that are not godly. What do I do? I repent and I ask God to cleanse my heart and my mind. Only He can make those changes as long as I am willing to undergo the process. Sometimes, I have to go back to the drawing board and evaluate myself. What caused me to react that way? What am I dealing with inside that I have not allowed God to handle? What godless emotions do I need to release? It could be resentment, unforgiveness, disappointment or pain. I sit before God and surrender it all to Him so He can truly break those chains from me and I can walk in complete victory.

The fire is surely uncomfortable and sometimes just seems plain hard, but I encourage you to stand strong, endure and fully depend on God in that holding place. One thing is for sure, the heat and the challenges in your life are there to change your climate and create a new atmosphere. Your passion for the things of God will increase and your focus will shift to where it needs to be. Many times, we can allow ourselves to just get distracted unintentionally. God has to turn up the heat to remind us that He is our center. After a while, there will be a reward; you will come out stronger, better, and wiser than you were before.

Chapter 7

THE BEAUTY IN THE BREAKING

"God uses broken things. It takes broken soil to produce a crop, broken clouds to give rain, broken grain to give bread, broken bread to give strength. It is the broken alabaster box that gives forth perfume" – Unknown

The times will come in your life when you face heartaches, setbacks, and disappointments. Life will just feel like it's hard. Maybe someone close left you and you don't know what to do. You may feel like everyone is against you in life. It's not easy but these moments don't come to kill you; rather, they make you stronger. Now, I know what you're thinking: "How can being hurt, mistreated, misunderstood, or just lost make me stronger? I feel weak; I feel worn; I feel like I can't trust again. I'm just over it."

Believe me when I say I've had my share of those thoughts as well. One thing I've learned is that my current thoughts are not my reality. How I feel at the moment is based on my present circumstance but how my story ends depends on how I choose to look at my situation. It is what I say during my storm and how I allow God to help me out of it.

A few times in my life, I have felt damaged and heartbroken. I just knew those who hurt me had shattered my dreams. At some point, I had envisioned myself getting married one of these individuals, blending our families, having children and all these "things." I was so fixed on these dreams that when the relationships ended, I felt that my promises from God went right along with them. What I learned from walking with God and overcoming that situation is that I should never place God's plan for my life in the hands of a person.

God's plan is sure for you. No matter what comes or goes, God is still God. His Word is still true, and it will never return unto Him void. That means even if someone hurts and walks away from you, the Lord can still keep His promise to you. Even if the person you thought would love you forever says they don't want you anymore, God's love is still present, and He still cares for you. His love isn't based on how another person feels about you.

    God's love does not waver based on a mistake you made; He doesn't walk off because you aren't performing in an area of your life. God is love, and He can never deny who He is. God is close to the brokenhearted and through your pain, your hurt, and your lowest times, He is able to show you the great power of His love. It is when everyone walks out on you that He is able to walk in, lift you up, hold you in His hands and shape you for His glory. I am very thankful for those moments now as I have such a great love relationship with God and an earthly love that makes my life so much better. The past no longer means a thing to me but a tool to catapult me into this blessed place I am in now.

He Builds the Broken Things

I've seen God take the most broken, bruised, battered, and unqualified people and with one touch transform them to the most powerful, purpose-filled, and passionate people. Nothing is impossible with God! We must remember that the coal mine is filled with many radiant, sparkling, shining diamonds that have not yet been introduced to their process of beautification. They're hidden in the ground in total darkness waiting to be discovered by those who know their value.

Listen, God knows your value if no one else does. He sees your potential. He knows your heart inside out. He has a purpose for you even in the midst of darkness. He's calling you out into His marvelous light. Don't allow any situation to make you forget your value. Don't let other people's inability to see your worth make you question your value to God and on this earth.

You are bought by God with a high price. He sent His Son Jesus to die on the cross for all of your sins and all of your brokenness and pain. I'm not saying you will never experience hurtful times because you will.

The good news is you don't have to remain there. You don't have to wallow in a hurtful place. You don't have to revisit that heartbreak time and time again in your mind. You can be free from hurt and pain by opening up your heart to God and allowing Him to come in and clean sweep your heart, mind, and spirit. I love the scripture that says, "God makes everything beautiful in its time" (Ecclesiastes 3:11). It helps me to remember that beauty means process.

The flower starts out as a seed in the ground, and it flourishes in the right season. How unfortunate would it be to have a handful of beautiful sunflower seeds that have the potential to blossom into strong, brilliant, yellow sunflowers but you throw them away because you do not understand the process and the timing? Don't be that person who cannot receive a promise because you don't recognize the need for the process or because you continue to quit in the middle.

The Word of God tells us to continue on because there will be a reward for those who refuse not to give up. "Let us not become weary in doing good for at the proper time we will reap a harvest if we do not give up" (Galatians 6:9, NIV). In other words, if someone hurts you, continue to love that person in spite of how you feel. Someone may have taken advantage of your kindness at some point or another but don't stop helping people because of a negative experience. Even things that come to set you off track or hurt you will work together for your good if you just stay the course and continue to trust God.

You don't have to think of ways to "fight back" or repay anyone for what they may have done to you. God has it all under control. His ways are not your ways and His thoughts are not your thoughts. Pray for others without ceasing so that you can stay in a blessed place. When a diamond is broken, it doesn't stop being a diamond, it becomes two. Instead of seeing your brokenness as place of being bound, see it as a season of blessing to refocus and draw yourself nearer to God. It was in my broken-hearted days that I drew strength I never knew I had. I found peace that surpassed my own understanding. I found joy unspeakable and faith unstoppable. Now, when I face hard times, disappointments, or attacks, I get my mind on God and what He is doing in that time. I expect something to come from it all and it always does. Allow the breaking to humble you, build you, and fortify you from the inside out and know that God has a plan even in the valley.

Chapter 8

SHINE BRIGHT FOR HIS GLORY

"Don't shine so that others can see you, shine so that through you others can see HIM" – C.S. Lewis

The entire goal of our lives as believers is to bring God glory. Everything we go through in life will come down to hearing God say, "Well done thy good and faithful servant." Our lives exist for the glory of the Lord, not for ourselves. Make sure that once God begins to use you that it's always for His glory. He wants His children drawn to His heart. Each time I am asked to speak to a group of people whether to encourage or share my personal testimony, I ask God to shine bright and dim me. God uses people He can trust. Can God trust you? When He brings you out of a situation and sets your feet above ground will you tell others how good He is? Will you be ashamed to share it with people because of what they will think about you or what they have to say?

Be Free of People Bondage

Some people are in bondage to the opinions of others to the point where they are afraid to share anything God does for them. They don't want people to think of them differently so they remain silent. I think about the times I was persuaded to live for God because of other's testimonies of deliverance, blessings or just seeing someone's boldness to live for God without shame. Someone's confidence in God could be an inspiration to others who struggle with low self-esteem.

They may look and say, "How is that person so comfortable with who they are when I don't even like myself?" Maybe they need to hear that they are fearfully and wonderfully made. That scripture kept me strong many days when I was becoming a woman and going through so many changes physically and emotionally. It kept me from being tempted to compare myself to other people around me. It helped me when others didn't prefer things about me that I loved about myself.

We cannot be afraid to shine the light of God inside of us when this world is so dark, starving and in need of light. Many people will never attend your church; some won't crack open a Bible and read it but many will come across your path in various places. They will listen to what you have to say about life; some people will value your opinion just because of a position you hold either at work, school, in your organization or on your social network. Why not use your influence to help lift up another?

One day at work, I ran into a lady who was preparing to travel to a few states so her husband could have surgery on his eye. He'd gotten injured at work and was facing the possibility of being permanently blinded in his left eye. When I spoke with her, I couldn't help but pick up that she was highly worried and stressed out about the situation. She was very detailed with me about all that was happening, and I knew she needed to vent. I was more than happy to listen but I couldn't allow her to stay that way without showing her that she could trust in the power of God. I proceeded to say, "We will believe for complete healing in his eye."

I was able to share with her my own experience with one of my eyes that is now non-existent. She was encouraged by my story because it gave her some confidence and hope to believe the best for her husband's situation. As she was leaving, she gave me a hug and then out of nowhere, she grabbed my hand and asked me to come to her car and say a prayer for her and her husband as they traveled.

This lady had never met me before; she didn't know what church I attended or what denomination I belonged to. Something about our conversation encouraged her to ask me to speak to God on her behalf. What a privilege to be able to lead someone in prayer and help build their faith in God for a specific situation.

A Light Cannot Be Hidden

The light of God is unquenchable and you can't hide it. When you've been spending time with God in prayer, in solitude, in complete surrender to Him, He will shine through you. You won't have to make a grand announcement or draw attention to yourself. People will be drawn to God's love that lives on the inside of you. You will be able to have talks with people sharing God's Word without preaching a sermon. You will be able to enlighten others to the Word without always quoting scripture (although that is also good) it will just be a lifestyle. Others will pick up something about you that they will say is different. The difference will be the glory of the Lord shining.

It is a beautiful thing to be made whole and complete in the Lord after enduring trials, tribulations, setbacks, attacks, and challenges that ultimately made you stronger. It is great to be able to stand on the Word for any situation because you know your foundation is sure and safe. There is a saying, "Diamonds are a girl's best friend." I would say that isn't too far off, especially because if you are in Christ, you are His special jewel. His refined jewel.

You may find yourself in this process of refinement down in the dark valley, hurt, dismayed, confused, and trying to figure it all out. You are right where you need to be. Yes, you may be there but please don't stay there. Find your place on the road to refinement so you can stand up, continue on and allow God to do the work in you. Yes, it's tough; yes, it calls for changes, commitment, and being open to change. However, no matter where you might be today just know it will be worth it. You are worth it. God wants to shape, mold, and build you up to be His perfect masterpiece.

I will leave you with three assignments that will never fade away no matter what season you are in. They are from 1 Thessalonians 5:16-18: "Rejoice always, pray without ceasing, give thanks in all circumstances; for this is the will of God in Christ Jesus for you." Three simple actions: REJOICE, PRAY, AND GIVE THANKS! I would like to pray with you and for you as you complete this book that wherever you find yourself today, you will open your heart to God's move in your life.

PRAYER

Lord, I thank You for Your children. Continue to be with them, lead them, guide them, and direct their paths. May You strengthen their hearts, minds, and spirits with Your grace and goodness. Keep them focused on the path You have set before them. Give them complete confidence that You are always with them in every situation and every season. Remind them that You will never leave them or forsake them and that You will be with them always. We take hold of Your love, joy, wisdom, and peace that passes all understanding. We release everything from our hearts that may keep us bound. We release every feeling and emotion that is not like You and we receive everything You are. We thank You; we love You and we count it done. In Jesus' name, Amen.

Refined Reflections

I created this section to help you reflect, reinforce, and re-align what you read in "Refined Jewels." If you are like many, you retain information better by revisiting key points and jotting them down. Writing helps to sort out your thoughts and plans so you can walk out your refining process. Don't allow yourself to put this down as just another "good read" but an opportunity to put your learning into action. Grab a pen, a snack, and prepare to seal it with some reflection!

Kamisha

1. In what areas of my life am I being challenged and how can I use them to my advantage?

_____

_____

_____

_____

_____

_____

2. What is my perception of the challenges I am facing?

_____

_____

_____

_____

_____

3. What emotions do I need to submit to God to be refined and made better?

_____

_____

_____

_____

_____

4. What are some areas in my character that may need to be adjusted for me to reach another level?

_____

_____

_____

_____

_____

5. What situations am I facing right now that I may be trying to avoid or run from? How can I grow from them?

_____

_____

_____

_____

_____

6. What fears do I have that are limiting me from moving forward in this season?

_____

_____

_____

_____

_____

7. What are some distractions that need to be eliminated in my life? What steps am I willing to take in order to be free from those distractions?

_____

_____

_____

_____

_____

8. What tools am I using to strengthen my faith to stand during challenges? (Prayer, Word, Worship, Spiritual Leadership, Teachings, Serving, Journaling, Counseling).

_____

_____

_____

_____

_____

9. What can I do to help others in their times of need? Have I been aware of those around me who might need help or encouragement?

_____

_____

_____

_____

_____

10. What are some goals in my life for this year and how will I achieve those goals?

_____

_____

_____

_____

_____

GOAL #1:

___

___

___

STEP 1:

___

___

___

STEP 2:

___

___

STEP 3:

GOAL #2

STEP 1:

STEP 2:

STEP 3:

GOAL #3

_____

_____

STEP 1:

_____

_____

_____

STEP 2:

_____

_____

_____

STEP 3:

Refined Reflections

_____

_____

_____

Prayers

_____

_____

_____

Resources

I invite you to visit **KamishaLattimore.com** so you can be connected with blogs, posts, videos, and encouragement to keep you walking out your process!

I also recommend getting a great study Bible so you can become a student of God's Word. I always recommend getting a translation that is easy for you to understand. To always know the will and plan of God *for your life and your situation, it will require quality time in the Word so you can know what God has to say about your life!*

ABOUT THE AUTHOR

Kamisha Lattimore is a passionate young woman who is walking in her purpose. She is a writer, blogger, speaker, and creative who is fervent about living out God's Word. She is a graduate of Charleston Southern University and loves to encourage her generation to live bold, free, and unashamed for God. She is the author of the inspirational book *A Chosen Journey* and the creator of online resource House of Hannah. (www.KamishaLattimore.com)

www.ingramcontent.com/pod-product-compliance
Lightning Source LLC
LaVergne TN
LVHW051558070426
835507LV00021B/2634